492

The Inner Fire

The Inner Fire

Allen W. Brown

Word Books, Publisher
Waco, Texas

Contents

Preface

I had come increasingly to believe that some new things needed to be written about prayer when an opportunity presented itself in the form of an invitation to address the annual Anglican Fellowship of Prayer Conference scheduled to meet in Minneapolis in the spring of 1974. Meanwhile I was about to retire, and some fresh prayer literature was beginning to appear with the result that, Jonah-like, I rejected the invitation, only to discover that God does not let us off that easily. I was spending a few days in advance of the conference fishing in Montana when a call came through advising me that, for good reason, one of the principal addresses could not be given; would I act as a substitute speaker? Frankly, the last minute request came as no surprise.

The official conference theme, "Prayer and Evangelism Unite," suggested the format and content of an address which was done hurriedly but, I trust, not without a measure of inspiration. The original material has been reworked in the hope that it will speak not only to those whose prayer life is advanced, but also to those who may be confused about prayer or who do not pray at all.

This is no easy task because Christians these days have difficulty communicating with non-Christians. Unlike Jonah, I have no gourd tree beneath which to sit if I have failed, but if what I have written adds to the growing understanding of prayer and its possibilities, I shall rejoice.

ALLEN W. BROWN
Retired Bishop of Albany

The Feast of St. Michael and All Angels
1977

Acknowledgments

Appreciation is expressed to the following publishers and authors for permission to use quotations which appear in the course of this book:

Harper and Row, Teilhard de Chardin, *The Phenomenon of Man*, 1959.

"The Living Church," Simcox, an editorial.

The New York Times, Strong, an address at the United Nations.

Penguin Books, Ltd., Laing, *The Politics of Experience*, 1967.

Prentice-Hall, Symonds, *The Dynamics of Human Adjustment*, 1946.

The Reader's Digest, Carrell, "Prayer is Power."

Simon and Schuster, Barber, *The Night They Raided Minskys*, 1960.

State University College, Brockport, *Perspectives in Education, Religion and the Arts*, 1969.

The Church Pension Fund, *The Hymnal*, 1940.

Acknowledgments

To Helen Shoemaker for her encouragement, and to Keith Miller for his off-the-cuff remarks at the U.S. Conference on Evangelism in Minneapolis, 1969, quoted in chapter three. I also am grateful to the Anglican Fellowship of Prayer for its invitation to speak at its International Conference, also in Minneapolis, 1974; much of the book is based on an address prepared in response to that invitation.

Stir up the fire that is in you

—2 Timothy 1:6

The Dynamics of Prayer

15.00   John odrzinia

Zirane Excellence

W E J C ministry
W E J C-TV
P.O. B 49555
C. Box 27419

2 ting 16

Chapter One

The Dynamics of Prayer

The function of communication is to break down barriers; the result is creative action and mutual understanding. Prayer is essentially effective communication with God; its primary purpose is to create unity between man and God, but there are other consequences. Unity with God leads to growth in the interior unity of the one who prays and ultimately to an exterior unity with one's fellow human beings. Prayer always is interpersonal. It is dialogue rather than monologue, conversation, as Clement of Alexandria suggested, rather than soliloquy. Prayer is effective without being manipulative. As we shall see later it involves the release of energy and is above all else a process of relationship with God himself.

God is the one who initiates the process. Our awareness is in proportion to our response.

There are many misconceptions about prayer. The beginner is beset with the idea that prayer means only petition, the asking for things, and he is likely to picture it as a one-way activity with himself, rather than God, as the center. As one grows in the life of prayer, new discoveries will be accompanied by new but not insurmountable difficulties. Much patience is needed.

In conversation humans are inclined to chatter too much and to listen too little. Conversation always is a two-way process. "Be still," the Psalmist says, "and know that I am God" (Ps. 46:10). In all of life there are times to speak and times to refrain from speaking (Eccles. 3:7). The late Baron von Hügel, a distinguished lay theologian of a century ago, wrote that man's most fundamental need is the adoration of God. To wait silently in prayer is as important as to speak. As Elijah discovered, awareness is generally to be found in life's silences (1 Kings 19:11–18). To put it colloquially, we must give God equal time! Prayer is commonly thought of only in terms of asking— petition, supplication, and intercession. While care must be taken not to let a study of prayer get in the way of prayer itself, it will be helpful, nonetheless, to recognize the several kinds of prayer in terms of intention as well as techniques.

The commonly recognized kinds of prayer are (1) *Confession*, telling God we are sorry to have "missed the mark" (a common New Testament word for sin taken from the sport of archery), (2) *Petition*, asking on behalf of ourselves, (3) *Intercession*, asking on behalf of others, persons, situations, etc., (4) *Thanksgiving*, saying thank you to God, and (5) *Adoration*, closely related to meditation and consisting of being still to tell God we love him. Sometimes a sixth, *Praise*, is added, but it is actually a component of adoration and thanksgiving.

All prayer has social implications. Confession, adoration, and thanksgiving are essentially one-to-one relationships between God and the one who prays. And, if we take care to avoid the imagery of a three-story universe, it may be visualized as prayer in the perpendicular. Intercession and petition imply change in relationships as well as intervention and, with the same caution, may be thought of as prayer in the horizontal.

While the distinctions will be familiar to many readers, there are several techniques which ought to be recognized: (1) *Liturgical or Formal Prayer*, whether in the form of poetry (e.g. psalms and hymns) or prose (i.e. a liturgy or prayer book) and always involving group participation; the word *liturgy* literally means a "public work"! (2) *Personal Prayer*, whether in one's own words or the language of a book, (3) *Free Worship*, which like liturgy involves people but is non-stylized and informal, and (4) *Meditation*, which may consist of (a.) *pure silence*, (b.) *the repetition of a brief prayer word* or Mantra, which in Transcendental Meditation may be quite meaningless, but which for the Christian consists of short phrases such as the "Jesus Prayer," [1] the "Hail Mary," (Luke 1:28), or such sentences as "Jesus my Lord, I thee adore," "I am thy saviour, trust me," or (c.) *the disciplined application of the mind to a specific subject*, generally biblical, in four steps— What is it? What of it? How do I feel about it? and What am I going to do about it? [2]

As there are different kinds of prayer and different techniques men use when they pray, so also there are different theories as to how prayer operates. They may be classified, I trust not with irreverence, as—

1. the Santa Claus Theory,
2. the Great Magician Theory,

3. Dynamic Prayer, and
4. the concept of prayer as intercourse within an intimate and loving family relationship.

To conceive of God as a kind of cosmic Santa Claus with prayer as the letters petitioners address to him is not child-like, but childish. It seems to contradict the statement of Jesus, "Your heavenly Father knows of what things you have need before you ask him" (Matt. 6:8), and, in the case of unanswered prayer, poses three unpleasant possibilities—(a.) Perhaps I was a bad child (which you probably were). The implication here is that answers to prayer are something earned rather than the result of God's free goodness and grace (Matt. 20:15). (b.) Perhaps my letter was lost, a denial of God's capacity to hear and know; (c.) Perhaps there is no Santa Claus! Surely prayer as taught by Jesus and as practiced by holy men and women in many centuries is something of greater dignity than this! How tragic that faith is lost so frequently because the nature of prayer itself has been misunderstood!

To think of prayer in terms of the "Great Magician" is equally inadequate. Magic, of course, is something more than sleight-of-hand entertainment. It is the doctrine held by many persons, including Chris-

tians, that when the right person uses the right for-
mula (words, actions, or both) the supernatural has
no choice except to act. The question of what makes
for validity in traditional theology and the familiar
conclusion to many prayers, "We ask it in thy Name.
Amen." are sufficiently illustrative. It is not a denial
that God is personal, loving, and capable of intervention, or of the need for decency and order in the
church (1 Cor. 14:40) to suggest that to think of
God as a Master Magician or, worse, as the genie in
the bottle is both inadequate and blasphemous.

The promise of answer to prayer asked in Jesus'
name (John 14:13) does not imply that "in Jesus'
name" or "through Jesus Christ our Lord" are magic
formulae by which God can be manipulated. The
point of Jesus' teaching is that a prayer which we
have the right to expect to be answered must be
morally and spiritually compatible with the nature
of God.

It might be noted that God seems to act primarily
when our prayers relate to his creativity in what is
his universe. The statement "Gather up the fragments
that remain that nothing be lost" (John 6:12) likewise expresses the principle of conservation rather
than destruction of all that is God's handiwork. The
twin activities of creativity and conservation include

not only the visible and material order, but also intellectual, moral, and artistic achievement in the arena of human relationships which he has established.

To pray in his name implies that we are co-workers with a God who continues to work (John 5:17). The effectiveness of prayer includes not only what God does because he is God, but also the extension of our own limited but creative power. Those who have struggled in prayer know the experience of power going from them. "Who touched me?" Jesus asked, "For I perceive that power is gone out of me" (Mark 5:30). The biblical word is related to our English word *dynamic* as well as to *dynamo* and *dynamite!*

"Prayer is power," wrote Alexis Carrell, "a force as real as terrestrial gravity." [3] As the uniting of oxygen with that which is consumed produces fire, the turning of a dynamo, power and a nuclear reactor, energy, so the effectiveness of prayer, especially in intercession and petition, is a consequence not only of God's response to human need but also of the spiritual energy generated and expended by the one who prays. "We are workers together with him," St. Paul says (2 Cor. 6:1). To pray is part of our work (1 Thess. 5:17).

Prayer also has subjective consequences, but we

must not fall into the trap of reducing it to a kind of auto-suggestion. Prayer is power. Prayer is effective communication with God. Out of the interpersonal pattern of caring activity on the part of God, others, and the praying self proceed creative results.

> Prayer is the soul's sincere desire,
> Uttered or unexpressed,
> The motion of a hidden fire
> That glows within the breast.[4]

All analogies have their limitations, but if one accepts the idea that prayer is power, the Dynamo (or dynamic) Theory of prayer is consistent with the doctrine of creativity on God's part—of man, being somehow made in God's likeness, sharing in the process of creativity. This theory is in line with some new understandings of mental energy and is not inconsistent with biblical teaching. It is particularly helpful in dealing with the problem of unanswered prayer.

Several years ago a major electronics company[5] sponsored an exhibit which illustrated some new possibilities in the generation and broadcast of electric power. The display consisted of a hand-powered generator and a nearby antenna-equipped electric corn popper. When the crank on the generator was turned, power was generated and transmitted through the air, to be picked up by the antenna, transformed into heat, and the corn popper activated. This commonplace illustration may help us understand the part human energy plays in intercessory prayer. Our expenditure of energy is only part of the process, but those who intercede regularly testify that it is hard work and an enervating experience. St. Thomas Aquinas teaches that angels, having neither extension or dimension, do not occupy space and, therefore, are able to exercise their ministry by applying their power to the place or situation in which they wish to be.

A concept of prayer as power will help us in a world where God's will does not always seem to be done. Indeed the Bible does not teach that God's will is always and unfailingly done; if it did, the familiar phrase in the Lord's prayer, "Thy will be done on earth as it is in heaven" (Matt. 6:10) would be unnecessary and meaningless. That which makes heaven, heaven is the fact that, in contrast to earth, there God's will is done. "Thy will be done on earth *as it is in heaven!*" In the Book of Revelation, also known as the Apocalypse, we read that "the devil is come down having great wrath" (Rev. 12:12), and St.

Peter writes, "Be vigilant because your adversary, the devil, as a roaring lion walketh about seeking whom he may devour" (1 Peter 5:8). Most significant evidence of all is the fact that at the time of his temptation (Luke 4:6) Christ did not dispute satan's claim to lordship in the present world.

In the face of the disturbing probability that God's will is not always done, Christ enunciates three principles which will be helpful in our dilemma:

1. After acknowledging that God's will is not always done (Luke 4:6), he declares that, nonetheless, "thou shalt worship the Lord thy God and him only shalt thou serve."

2. He declares that nothing, however disastrous, can happen beyond the purview of God's love. "Are not five sparrows sold for two farthings, and not one of them is forgotten before God. . . . Fear not! You are of more value than many sparrows" (Luke 12:6–7).

3. He says there is one prayer guaranteed to be answered, that, if we meet the condition of obedience, God will surely give us the Holy Spirit (Luke 11:13).

The healing power of medicine is not able always to effect a cure, but we do not abandon medicine. There are mountains one's automobile is unable to climb, but we continue to drive. So sometimes the dynamic of prayer may be unequal to the task—which makes it the more important that we continue to pray, because the combination of the will of God and human effort is more effective than either exercised without the other.

After we have dealt with the three common understandings of prayer, acknowledging misconceptions in some areas and quite legitimate claims in others, we return to a fourth and important Christian concept of prayer—that of a loving relationship between a parent who understands and loves his children, although he may not and, perhaps sometimes cannot, accede to their requests, and children who, in return, not only have needs, but also a capacity to love. This is what Jesus meant when he taught his disciples to say "Our Father." And, as we shall see presently, it may explain what is meant when he says, "Unless you change and become as children you shall in no wise enter the kingdom of heaven" (Matt. 18:3).

Jesus and his disciples spoke an everyday Middle-

Eastern dialect known as Aramaic. Hebrew was the language of worship and of those formally educated, much as, until recently, Latin was the language of the Roman Catholic Church. Greek, on the other hand, was the common literary language of the Mediterranean world, somewhat as French has been the international language of Western culture. As a result of this multi-lingual system in the first century, some of the earliest portions of the Gospels may have been recorded in Aramaic, but the New Testament was written in Greek, not however without retaining patterns of Aramaic language and thought.[6]

The Aramaic word "Abba," which occurs only three times in the New Testament,[7] is a less formal word than its Greek or English translation "Father." It is the word our Lord always used in conversation and prayer. It is important that we remember this; otherwise the *intimacy* implied in the original Aramaic is lost.

In this life we never can fully comprehend the relationship between the dynamics of prayer and the limitations imposed as a result of God's having ordained natural law and free will, or, for that matter, the fact that he allows evil to exist. Perhaps it will help if we remember that were it otherwise, God would be Master Puppeteer, and we should be slaves rather than sons. The important and never-to-be-forgotten relationship remains— He is "Our Father" (Abba), and we are sons (Gal. 4:6, 7).

The early Christians knew persecution (John 16:2) and were well aware that the rain falls alike on the unjust and the just (Matt. 5:45). They also believed that while Jesus was their "great high priest ascended into the heavens," he was also one sensitive to human need because he had been subject to it (Heb. 4:14, 15). They knew, as Christians in every generation have discovered, that, "the earnest, glowing prayer of a righteous person availeth much" (James 5:16), and when their efforts seem inadequate they remember that the Holy Spirit, also, is involved in outreach beyond the capacity of human ears to comprehend or language to express (Rom. 8:26). Thus Christians continue to pray in the face of problems, injustice, and pain because they know Whom it is that they trust.

Prayer Unites

Chapter Two

Prayer Unites

Jesus said, "No man can do a miracle in my name and then lightly speak evil of me" (Mark 9:39). Because prayer works miracles, those who pray find themselves growing in union with God, developing integrity or wholeness within themselves, and, without always agreeing theologically, developing a fresh sense of oneness with their fellow human beings. The unifying aspects of prayer ultimately may prove to be important in man's final destiny.

The religious mind, instinctively conservative, is forever struggling with new ideas—only to discover eventually that the data, which at first seemed to threaten, in reality was part of God's total truth previously unrecognized. Thus it is that the universe of Galileo, Copernicus, Magellan, and the astronauts

proclaims a creation more majestic than could have
been imagined by Ptolemy, the apostles, or the author
of that part of the Old Testament sometimes referred
to as "The J Document." [8]

The details of creation are clothed in mystery; time
itself is quite beyond human understanding. The
tendency is to over-simplify. Many devout Christians
believe that the "days" referred to in the Book of
Genesis describe eras of time rather than neat twenty-
four hour periods and find support for such belief
in the Psalms. One attributed to no less a person than
Moses illustrates,

A thousand years in thy sight are but as yesterday
    when
it is past, and as a watch in the night (Psalm 90:4).

The future, however, is more important than the
past, and however God saw fit to effect his creation
and its ongoingness, the fact remains that living
things, if they are to survive and develop, must forever adjust to their environment. This is more than a
matter of biology; it is a spiritual necessity if man is to
find his true environment.

Prayer unites man with God, man within himself,

and persons one with another. We shall consider them in that order. In each instance prayer, rightly understood, is the process.

Fish are at home in the water because they have adapted to their environment; similarly birds are at home in the air and animals on dry land. Within limits man lives in the water, the air, and on dry land, but a physical environment is never totally adequate to his needs; he is in but, unlike other creatures, not of it. Man's true environment is God, in whom he lives and moves and has his being (Acts 17:28). Man's torturous history reflects the process of his learning to relate to his true environment. Prayer, therefore, is not something to be added to lives already complicated, but is the unifying and necessary action through which man relates to God. It is no easy process. As in other processes of adaptation, it is marked by trial and error, progress and failure, and, if "fitness" is understood as the willingness to respond, by a survival of the fittest. Sometimes this learning to live in God is unconscious until a sudden awareness reveals that progress has been made. Sometimes, because man has the capacity to make choices, the development is self-conscious and deliberate, but always it is in the nature of response. Man does not "find" God.

Man, not God, is lost until he learns to live in his true environment—which is God.

St. Augustine's "Thou, O God, hast made us for thyself, and our souls are restless until they find rest in thee" is quoted universally because it speaks to man's universal condition and experience. It appears that, while many creatures have a limited capacity to think, man alone knows that he thinks, which means that he operates on a higher and different level of consciousness. Likewise, as far as we know, he alone is capable of prayer (and praise) which is the conscious response of created to creator. The result is that as he becomes aware of his environment, he he moves towards his ultimate destiny, at-one-ment with God. The word *atonement* popularly suggests some kind of transaction, but etymologically it means a transformation from isolation (Rom. 12:2) to union with God.

Union with God, then, is more than a technical religious experience. It is also more than a privilege or an obligation intended exclusively for the devout. Union with God is man adapting to the only environment which can satisfy his ultimate need. Prayer is the medium through which man relates to this environment. Prayer, therefore, is neither an avocation for people otherwise engaged in important things, nor an extra burden imposed upon already busy lives, but the business of life itself!

The prayer that unites man with God presupposes certain conditions, some intellectual, some moral and social, some theological. "He that cometh to God must believe that he is" (Heb. 11:6). Note well the word is *believe* not *prove*. Belief is not certainty which means "It is certain," but *certitude* which means "I am certain." Certitude is the basis not only of religion but also of all belief. There is very little of which it may be said "It is certain," as we are reminded by the contrast in our contemporary understanding of the atom with that which scientists believed a century ago. Certitude means weighing the evidence, accepting the observed results, and acting accordingly. Subsequent experience becomes part of the total data—either reinforcing the original conclusion, or demanding a reassessment of the previous judgment. Belief, in the sense of certitude, is something quite different from credulity, or blind belief, which thoughtful persons rightly refuse to accept. It is the responsible conviction of a disciplined mind.

The record of those who have known God best

indicates other conditions which must be met if one is to move from what sometimes is called the Purgative Way, through the Illuminative Way, until the life of union with God is attained. These conditions include an honest heart (Ps. 51:10), or, as the New Testament puts it, "the single eye" (Matt. 6:22); a receptive attitude (John 1:8, 9); the practice of justice (Mic. 6:8); a concern for the poor,[9] and a right relationship with one's fellow human beings (Matt. 5:24)—including a non-manipulative attitude in matters of sex (Gal. 3:28).

The Christian also sees union with God as growing out of a basic unity with Christ (John 14:20, John 15), especially in the action of the Eucharist (John 6:56, 57) and always related to the activity of the Holy Spirit.

Prayer which unites man with God manifests itself in a number of ways. Sometimes it is a matter of quiet, unspoken dialogue; sometimes it is the cataclysmic experience of a burning bush (Exod. 3:1–6), a Temple vision (Isa. 6), or a conversion on the Damascus road (Acts 9:3–4). The awareness may occur in the marketplace, but it is experienced more often in disciplined listening, which is why extended silence is important in prayer. It was in the paradox of a silence so deep as to be heard that God spoke to Elijah (1 Kings 19:12). It was in silence that Job discovered both his humanness and the answer to his need (Job 1:6). In the violence of Psalm 46 God speaks, "Be still and know that I am God" (Ps. 46:10), and the psalmist obeys—to discover himself in the silence surrounded by the presence of God.

Awareness of God through prayer not only leads to a sense of oneness with him but also to the discovery and development of one's personhood and integrity. There is a story about the father who, after the traditional long day's work, returned home, and, after dinner, sat down to read his newspaper only to be interrupted continually by a six-year-old son. Quite by chance he came upon a map of the world which, in an attempt to be let alone, he tore out, cut into several pieces, and gave to the boy as a puzzle to solve. To his amazement, the map was reassembled in a very few minutes. When asked how he could do this so quickly the boy replied, "Daddy, it was easy; there was a picture of a man on the other side, and when I put the man together, the world was all right!"

This modern parable says something about man's situation. In spite of rapid travel, instant communication, and unprecedented technical skill, man's world, including himself, has fallen apart. Later we shall think about prayer as a unifying force in society, but it is obvious that if humankind is to find unity, we must begin with the individual himself.

In the previous section we were considering prayer in the perpendicular, an image admittedly not without limitations, and have seen that prayer serves, among other things, to unite man with God. We continue the perpendicular image, but this time the direction is inward. Jesus said, "The kingdom of heaven is within you" (Luke 17:21).

However we describe it, the fact is that in man's development, something happened to man himself. He lost an integrity he might have had; the simple unity with which he began was broken, perhaps not once but several times. As a consequence his wholeness and natural harmony have become impaired, which is what theologians mean by "original sin." Original sin has nothing to do with sex under an apple tree. Unfortunate popular preaching on Psalm 51 ("In sin hath my mother conceived me") (Ps. 51:5) has thrown us off the track. The sexual revolution of the seventies may be, in part, overreaction to some extremely bad homiletics. Original sin is man's failure to move on from innocence to virtue at that time in his development when such an advance was, and continues to be, necessary; there is a sense in which each human being relives the experience of the race. This is man's inheritance, and the result always is the same —expulsion from his Eden and the loss of his integrity. Integrity, as we shall see later, is more than moral uprightness; it is that inner unity without which direction is lost. The result not only is confusion, but rebellion, frustration, and uncertainty that the self exists. "The wages of sin is death" (Rom. 6:23). "O wretched man that I am," St. Paul goes on to say, "who shall rescue me from this imperfection?" (Rom. 7:24). In addition to man's shattered personhood, external, but derived, factors conspire to acerbate his dilemma—the complexity of human society, the myriad forces which seek his loyalty, the breakdown in Western theology, and the secularization of life itself. Are we listening? Man needs help in putting himself together again. In its better moments this is what the church always has meant by redemption.

A century ago the Western mind thought in terms of escorting God to the rim of his universe, thanking him (as someone said) for past favors, and dismissing him as no longer relevant. Contemporary man has discovered, to his grief, that human progress is no "operation bootstrap." A hundred Buchenwalds remind us that Dr. Coué was wrong and that "day by day, in every way, man does not grow better and better." Without God, man is a lonely pilgrim in an alien universe. The "Death of God" of a decade ago led not to the deification of man but to his meaninglessness. Man lives because, to use the ancient Hebrew name for God, "The One Who Is" is verb as well as noun (Ex. 3:14).

A contemporary writer suggests that the condition of being out of one's mind has become the normal situation for modern man.[10] Certainly the inconsistency between man's behavior and his rhetoric indicates that something within has gone wrong. If he is not out of his mind, he is, at best, fragmented and in need of being put together again. Morally, the antonym for simplicity is not maturity but duplicity. The exile from Eden is essentially an inner thing because it is within that breakdown has occurred. Man's inability to reconstruct his fallen nature, however we may visualize it, is what redemption and restoration are all about. It is here that the unifying action of prayer, as *effective* communication, comes in. The chain reaction of evil, a phrase which should be understood by atomic man, was neutralized by Christ's death and resurrection and a new life process begun.[11] The casual Christian usually thinks of the new life in Christ in terms of quantity—"living forever," forgetting that the content of the "new life" is the important thing.

In the prayer process, man can rediscover his lost integrity, but it is a demanding and time-consuming exercise, and there are some preliminary steps he must take—first, he must recognize his need, a difficult thing for Western man, particularly for North Americans who have inherited the self-sufficiency philosophy of the pioneers. Horatio Alger heros may succeed in the competition of commerce, but, unless a redemptive element is added, they end up as the Laphams and Babbitts of society; as far as man's interior life is concerned there are no self-made men. The recognition of man's need leads to a willingness to accept help from outside and beyond one's self. St. Paul learned this, not without difficulty (Rom. 7:19–25). As we discover our own spiritual helplessness, we are moved to put everything in the hands of God. Openness becomes possible only as the barriers we have erected are taken down. Then and only then can the unifying action begin. One will observe a parallel in this personal awareness of need and the first steps in Alcoholics Anonymous. The "fast closed door" of the hymn [12] can be opened only from within.

Prayer serves to create new self-integrity because, as one continues to pray, old anxieties, fears, and destructive attitudes, as a consequence of grace [13] begin to disappear. The one in need who takes time to pray, who prays and listens, begins to discover a fresh awareness of God's presence and reality. There is a paradox in all this—curiously, the more one is aware of God, the less he is aware of himself, and yet as he loses self in the process, he rediscovers his own identity. [14]

As we allow the Holy Spirit to work in us, our prayer life expands; tensions give way to trust, frustration to hope, self-pity to concern for others. A new pattern of life begins to emerge, a life which has concern for others as well as concern for ourselves.

One must take care not to limit the work of the Spirit; he will not let us box him in! Without attempting to restrict the steps in an integrating prayer process, they include, not always necessarily in this order:

1. recognition of need,
2. willingness to accept help from outside,

3. an attitude of openness or honesty,
4. the loss of destructive attitudes,
5. a growing awareness of God,
6. less concern about self,
7. the unification of personhood (integrity),
8. improved attitudes,
9. better relationships with others,
10. the spiritual gifts of peace, love, joy.

The one who prays will make additional discoveries of his own.

As has been noted, one of the common New Testament words for sin is *harmatia*, a Greek word belonging to the sport of archery, which means "missing the mark." Man misses the mark. Divine action gets him back on target. Prayer keeps him there!

Wendell Wilkie wrote in 1937 of "one world"; the post-World War II generation became accustomed to two worlds, one "communist," one "free." With the passing of colonialism and the emergence of the lesser-developed nations, there now are three. Is there still a way to reunite mankind?

The situation is not promising. Ecumenism has brought many of the families within a divided Christendom closer together, but new patterns of theological separation have emerged; fundamentalism, for example, increasingly rejects ecumenism as the mouthpiece of an apostate liberalism, and new issues such as the ordination of women, social action, and liturgical revision threaten to create new schism even as older divisions disappear. More than religious loyalties are involved. An older generation which believed itself forward-looking in racial matters finds its position rejected by what may be minority leadership on both sides, but a leadership which is uncompromising, articulate, and given to violence. Moslem and Christian are far from peace in so ideal a Middle Eastern nation as Lebanon. There are signs of a break-through in Israeli-Arab relationships, but peace has not yet come, and, meanwhile, men and women create new movements under the banner of liberation movements that have their own intolerance and serve to divide further.

What can unite man with his fellow man? Certainly not the structured church, necessary as structure may be, not councils of churches nor United Nations, valuable as these agencies may be.

Welcome as Constantine's conversion was to a persecuted church, it resulted in a secularization of Christianity and a loss of the kind of unity proclaimed by the first century Christian community. History cannot be rewritten, but it is always possible to take a fresh look at beginnings. Is there a New Testament alternative to the ongoing fragmentation of humankind?

Jesus' way was not to challenge structures and programs but to see them in proper perspective, not as ends in themselves but as means to legitimate objectives. The Jesus way was and is a way of union, through him with the Father. The Jesus prayer is "That they all may be one; as thou, Father, art in me, and I in thee, that they also may be one with us" (John 17:21). "The kingdom of heaven," he said, "comes not with observation; the kingdom of heaven, i.e. the ideal, is within" (Luke 17:21). St. Paul, referring specifically to the division between Jew and Gentile, lays down the universal principle that, "He is our peace, who hath made both one, and hath broken down the middle wall of partition between us" (Eph. 2:14).

Prayer is communication, not just conversation; it is dynamic relating, not merely rubric and rite. The process may be pictured as a wheel with Christ as the center and praying persons as the spokes. As we draw nearer to him, we inevitably draw nearer to one another, and as we draw nearer one another, we draw nearer to him.

Communication by itself not only breaks down barriers but also creates them! The prayer that unites man with his fellow man is more than communication; it is communication in love. It begins with forgiveness, "If thou art offering thy gift at the altar and rememberest that thy brother hath aught against thee, leave there thy gift (Drop it!); first be reconciled with thy brother; then come and offer thy gift" (Matt. 5:24). Until we forgive we are unable to care; until we care we are unable to love. Until we love we are unable to intercede; until we intercede we are unable to pray. Until we pray we shall not discover that we are one.

The Old Testament generally emphasizes both racial and religious separateness, a separateness which often is misunderstood and sometimes deliberately misinterpreted. It is doubtful if the Jewish people and the doctrine of monotheism they were called to proclaim could have survived except for their sense of apartheid, which kept them from being absorbed by the surrounding paganism of the Middle East. To study this separateness is to discover that at its best Judaism recognized itself to be quite as much subject to judgment as neighboring nations and regarded having been called to be a "chosen people" not as a sign of superiority but as destiny for fulfillment of a purpose, the ultimate restoration of man's unity with God, lost by Adam's fall.

Christianity inherited this sense of separateness. St. Peter writes, "You are a chosen generation, a royal priesthood, a holy nation" (1 Pet. 2:9). It took an internal struggle within the First Century Church before Christians recognized the principle that, "God hath made of one blood all nations of men for to dwell on the face of the whole earth" (Acts 17:26). While Christians as individuals regrettably have displayed the kind of prejudices common to most mankind, when they do so they do not represent the church. The initial missionary thrust was not as much to save souls from hell (which literally means being cut off—isolated) as to proclaim the good news of a Messianic kingdom in which all would be one in Christ (Gal. 3:26–28).

Christian love, in the sense of *agape* (1 Cor. 13) was something new as distinct from both the brotherly love (*phileo*) one may have for his friends and family and the sexual attraction of nature (*eros*). Christian love proclaimed a unity with all human beings, an unselfish caring, more concerned with the needs of others than one's own. It is significant that no word exists which literally translates the unique concept of *agape*, that is "Christian love." It is more than tolerance, more than respect, more than being non-manipulative. On the purely human level such a way of life is as difficult to live as it is to define. It comes about only as in prayer the self-centeredness which is at the root of all our difficulties is overcome. It is a way of living and feeling which is given rather than achieved.

This unity, effected by prayer, is more than a subjective reaction. There is a creative, transforming factor in prayer which makes for a healing of the divisions which fragment relationships. Subtle changes occur as we pray; it is difficult to pray for someone and then speak evil of him. A prominent educator wrote in 1946, "The intellect is rarely used by persons in meeting the larger problems and issues of life. . . . The larger part of adjustment (to others) is carried on through the impulses, emotions, and similar mechanisms." [15] In prayer such ingredients as forgiveness, love, caring, clarity of vision, and the abandoning of pride effect a change in our priorities and attitudes. The dynamics at work in prayer unite and can result in a change of relationships between husbands and wives, employers and employees, members of special interest groups, and racial, political, and ideological antagonists. When its power to unite is recognized, prayer becomes an intensely practical thing.

The Director of the U. N. Environmental Program wrote a few months ago, "For the first time we have a situation in which the moral, philosophical, spiritual insights of the great religious leaders of the world, which used to be thought of as fuzzy-minded idealism —concepts of brotherhood, caring and sharing—now are preconditions of survival." [16]

The Night They Raided Minsky's was not a religious play, but some readers will remember a particularly poignant scene in which the senior Minsky, standing and wearing his yarmulke, and the Amish father, kneeling with his broad black hat in hand, pray together for the daughter's safe return. One of the actors bursts unannounced into the room. "Have you no decency," the elder Minsky asks, "disturbing two men of God at their prayers?"

The uniting power of prayer transcends creedal affirmations and liturgical practice. The strength of all brotherhood movements is not in their resolutions and pronouncements, their unity services and their study programs, but in their commitment to prayer.

Because prayer is so important a unifying force in human experience, something must be said about it in terms of the future of mankind. Teilhard de Chardin wrote, "No evolutionary future awaits man except in association with all other men." [17] He sees a new "layer" enveloping the world, a layer as distinct as the earth's surface, vegetation, atmosphere, animal life, or neolithic man. The psychologist Jung seems to hint at something similar in his phrase "group subconscious."

The union of man with his fellow man begins, then, to be seen as something more than idealism and rhetoric. Serious thinkers see the next step in man's long history as something more personal than a highly organized social structure, more meaningful than an invisible but conscious cloud of knowing, and more significant than a race of supermen. To quote Teilhard de Chardin again, he coins a word, *noosphere*, to describe this "organic super-aggregation of souls." [18] As has been said before, our language is inadequate; others have suggested other words. St. Paul put it well when he said, "We shall not be clothed but clothed upon" (2 Cor. 5), and St. John wrote,

"It doth not yet appear what we shall be" (1 John 3:2). Because prayer is a communication it is important in the ongoing unification of mankind.

> Sincere prayer for each other has great power because by cleaving to God in prayer I become one spirit with him, and unite myself, by faith and love, with those for whom I pray. The Holy Ghost acting in me acts at the same time in them. He accomplishes many things, and we being many are one body, one bread.[19]

Effective Sharing

Chapter Three

Effective Sharing

The word *catalyst* and the New Testament word *reconcile* are related.[20] This may help us understand the urgency about evangelism. "God was in Christ reconciling the world unto himself" (2 Cor. 5:19). Evangelism is sharing this good news, extending Christian horizons, proclaiming Christ as God's catalyst who creates change in human life, its understandings, values, and relationships. As prayer leads to evangelism, the need to share, so evangelism leads others to prayer, and prayer, in turn, to union with God, the unification of the self, and the uniting of persons with one another. It is an interrelated and ongoing process. The consequences of evangelism have such spiritual, personal, and social significance that the Christian sees them not as an "extra" or option but the great imperative calling for obedience, action, and sometimes personal risk.

Some years ago I found it necessary to make a plane connection in the middle of the night. The airport was small in those days, and I took refuge in the coffee shop occupied by two other travellers. It was not necessary to be an eavesdropper to discover quickly that they were talking about Jesus Christ. One was listening politely, interjecting an occasional question or comment; the other was talking about solutions he had found in his own life as a result of his faith in Jesus. His testimony was warm, enthusiastic, straight-forward, not without a kind of New Testament quality. To share the Good News was so urgent a matter to early Christians that they saw in each new situation a God-given opportunity to talk about the risen Lord and what life in him meant.

I listened, I confess, not without embarrassment, because I knew that I, a bishop, was not doing the kind of evangelism I heard taking place. In these days bishops are pastors, administrators, and presidents of a worshiping community, but outside the security of their pulpits, they seldom witness to their personal faith in Jesus Christ. This is not as it was in the beginning. St. Matthias, the first "bishop" to be chosen by the Apostolic Church, was nominated that he might be a witness to the resurrection (Acts 1:22). Pray, do not be too harsh with us; the assignment to make disciples belongs to every Christian; it is not something the laity hires the ordained clergy to do! St. Stephen, who did some effective early evangelism, was a deacon; the seventy who went out on the first preaching mission were laymen (Luke 10), and in every generation God has called a variety of persons to witness, regardless of their age, status, or sex.

Handicaps Along the Horizontal

The author of the Epistle to the Hebrews exhorts Christians to get rid of every handicap in their race for Christian achievement (Heb. 12:1). The biblical words are interesting, suggesting a runner who either is overweight or who gets tangled up in his uniform. Allusion already has been made to the language difficulties in spiritual communication, but there are other reasons why twentieth century Christians find themselves handicapped with evangelism and with what used to be called "missionary effort." Part of the difficulty is personal—lack of individual faith and commitment, neglect of Holy Scripture, and the quite illogical assumption that "One religion is as good as another." Some regard an attempt to interfere with another's religion as bad manners. Others make the non-biblical assumption that by good deeds, or, at least the avoidance of bad deeds, one builds up points for the future. Other road blocks are a fear of being thought "peculiar" or overly pious, the problem of vocabulary and symbols, the church's own record of divisiveness, and misconceptions about the Christian life itself.

There are not less than five major obstacles to effective evangelism; it will be helpful to recognize them:

1. the problem within society as a whole: communication,
2. the problem within the total Christian community: divisions,
3. the problem of those concerned about evangelism: a bad image,
4. the problem of the individual Christian: faith and practice,
5. the problem of leadership: confusion about priorities.

The problem of communicating the gospel to society as a whole is one with which the church always must reckon. Communication includes both language and concern. We shall deal with them separately.

If to survive, man must adapt to his environment, which is God, evangelism is essential to the ongoingness of human life itself, but this must be communicated as something more sophisticated than mere avoidance of a medieval hell.

The most accurate meaning of hell is a state of total separation from God himself; its essential quality is not the imagery of poets and Puritans but the irreversible fact of estrangement (2 Cor. 1:9). Our inability to describe the Jurassic landscape does not make the dinosaur any less extinct. Similarly, our inability to adequately describe the consequences of alienation from God does not make the condition of the soul, described as hell, any less disastrous.

The same must be said about any description of heaven. Modern man does not find golden streets and an eternity of hymn singing particularly inviting. The joy of heaven is in its unity, its fulfillment, its wholeness, in short, its integrity. Its meaning is qualitative. Again, language, at its best, is a poor attempt to express the inexpressible, to describe that which human language is inadequate to describe.

Harry Emerson Fosdick, a somewhat radical clergyman of a generation ago, used to emphasize the need for a kind of "urban renewal" in the language of evangelism. He pointed out that old buildings sometimes had to be torn down or maintained only as historic landmarks if new structures were to be built. This is no denial of basic truth. It does point out, however, that it is only in dead languages that meanings do not change, and that in living language words frequently change or lose their persuasiveness. To proclaim the Good News in living language calls for courage to recognize the problem, to avoid rigidity, and, while maintaining a sense of history, to present eternal truth in contemporary terms. The meaning of Pentecost is both proclamation and the power to interpret that persons may hear "in their own language the wonderful works of God" (Acts 2).

When the International Philosophical Year was observed in 1969, more than one speaker observed that philosophy had fallen into disrepute because, "Philosophers no longer spoke to anyone except other philosophers." [21] To proclaim the gospel in what is essentially a secular century, Christians must take care lest they fall into the same trap.

To continue only to talk cozily with one another

is to bury our talents and to invite judgment on the part of our Lord, who commissioned us not only to preserve but also to proclaim (Matt. 28:19–20).

Have we the courage to deal with the problems which arise in the minds of men geared to the century in which we live? To acknowledge our failures? To recognize that Christian thought has not kept pace with secular discovery? The cause will not be served by ignoring the difficulties, by staying in our private ghettos, or by being judgmental about those who do not believe. It may be that failure to extend our horizons makes modern men reject both prayer and the One to whom we pray.

Some readers will remember Keith Miller's dramatic interruption of his address in Minneapolis a few years ago. Miller, a well known lay-theologian, was scheduled to speak to the U. S. Congress on Evangelism. His audience, numbering perhaps five thousand practicing Christians, was made up of persons generally committed to sharing the "Jesus message" with others in such a way that non-believers would be moved to acknowledge him as Lord.

It was a time in American history marked by occasional riots, frequent demonstrations, and something close to revolution on many campuses; the auditorium was not without its own "security." As the speaker was introduced, two young people, a bearded and beaded young man and his female companion who had been floor-sitting at the front of the hall, were officially escorted out—apparently as a safety measure, regrettably, not without a few catcalls from the audience.

When quiet was restored, Miller came forward, laid his notes on the lectern, and began by saying:

> Ladies and gentlemen, the theme of my address was to have been that Christians talk only to other Christians, that we are unwilling or incapable of communicating with others. . . . A few minutes ago a young man who looked more like Jesus Christ than anyone I have seen at this meeting and his friend were thrown out of this auditorium. Unless these young people are returned, my thesis will have been demonstrated, and I shall have nothing to say!

There was a stunned silence, a tremendous awareness of personal and collective guilt. After a brief delay, the ushers returned the couple, to a standing ovation, and the address continued.

Extending the Horizons

Biblical religion always includes caring and sharing, which is another way of saying: prayer, social action, and evangelism. The thoughtful reader will discover several levels of revelation, or development, in the matter. It is a far cry from the primitive command to exterminate one's enemies (1 Sam. 15) to Jesus' "Love thine enemies; bless them that curse you; do good to them that hate you, and pray for them that despitefully use you and persecute you" (Matt. 5:44). The shift can be observed in the Old Testament in which such books as Joshua, Judges, Samuel, Ezra, and Kings are marked by extreme racial exclusiveness, and Israel's God seems concerned only with the well-being of Israel. The Torah, on the other hand, in its later form is concerned with justice for Jew and Gentile alike (Deut. 5:15). The Book of Ruth was written to reinforce this new understanding of inclusiveness, making the point that King David's own grandmother was a Moabitess. Jonah goes further—not only is God's compassion not limited to Israel, but Israel, symbolized by Jonah, has a mission to the heathen. It might be noted that Jonah himself was not entirely in sympathy with his message and was disappointed at the success of his preaching. The Prophetic Books generally express a belief in God's concern for all mankind, teaching that it is the responsibility of the Jew to share his knowledge of God with the non-Jewish world.

While Jesus' earthly ministry was confined generally to the Jewish community, he was not without Gentile contacts and saw his role as a messiahship for all mankind. He was as much at home with the lowly as with the professionally religious. St. Mark observes that the common people, more aware of their needs than the scrupulous and self-satisfied, heard him gladly (Mark 12:37). He taught that neighborliness was not a matter of race or position but of need (Luke 10:33). His disciples were not to keep their insights to themselves but to share them with all humanity (Matt. 5:13–14). As a consequence, Christianity became an intensely missionary-minded, proselytizing religion. It could not have been otherwise and remained true to itself and to its founder.

Courage to share, therefore, requires willingness to wrestle with the problem of communication and also a recognition that to reach outward includes intercessory prayer as well as evangelism. To intercede is to act as a "go-between," not to intercept, but to make a connection. Intercessory prayer, as already suggested, is energy expended not in telling God that which he already knows (Matt. 6:32) but in projecting love and self-sharing power on the part of the intercessor.

It is this kind of sharing, not without spiritual risks, which brings out mature, responsible effort on the part of the one who shares and also challenges those who have rejected religion as ingrown, defensive, and self-serving.

Perhaps two final illustrations may be given—man is always limited by his own understanding and vocabulary. Any experience of that which is beyond normal everyday experience must be described in and expressed by language which has validity for the one who has had the experience. The up and down traffic on Jacob's ladder (Gen. 28:10–17) records a communication experience but is not a treatise on astronomy. So a first century understanding of the universe does not invalidate the essential truth of what commonly is called "the Ascension" (Acts 1:9–10). Modern man probably would have used the phrase "back into" rather than "up," but if a man of the first century were to be recorded as having used such language, it would lead one to suspect that someone had tampered with the evidence.

Courage to share, then, requires knowledge and honesty on the part of the one who would share and openness on the part of those who casually dismiss the gospel.

Toward a Better Performance Record

The divisions of Christendom are a matter of concern to the total Christian community. This is no plea for an easy church unity, but rather an admission that our divisions, in themselves, are a denial of the power of prayer to unite. It will be helpful to distinguish between a political structure, once known as "Christendom" and the church itself. The kingdom of God, while not of this world (John 18:36), is a visible structure. Jesus said, "I will build my church" (Matt. 16:18) and made it quite clear that the identifying characteristic of his church was a supernatural unity in love (John 17:21). Ecumenism is here to stay and is something more significant than earlier attempts to create a secular "Super-church," a goal fortunately now abandoned as Christians are led into a loving recognition that the things they hold in common are greater than the things that divide. Individual Christians can help by prayer, by the avoidance of any downgrading of another's practice, by acknowledging their responsibility for our continuing divisions, and by recognizing with von Hügel that "To lack charity is the greatest of all heresies."

The bad image some people sometimes give the gospel is another encumbrance. The Good News must not be presented as a threat, another burden to be borne, or as Bad News. Something of the Puritan, unfortunately, lingers in the thinking of most Western Christians, with the result that whatever is interesting, colorful, and fun is presented as of the devil, and only that which is dull, dour, and drab as belonging to God. Unlike John the Baptist, the Lord Jesus Christ was warm and outgoing; he was one with whom persons liked to share their good times (Luke 7:33, 34). To make others uncomfortable makes for poor performance in either prayer or evangelism and is a sign of spiritual pride. Evangelism is everybody's business, but as we go about it we frequently should read and reread 1 Corinthians 13. Even clergymen sometimes joke a bit about their fellow clergy if they seem "too holy and pious." There is nothing wrong with being holy and pious; indeed, that is what God intends us to be! The difficulty is that holy and pious people sometimes give piety a bad name.

The individual Christian has his own responsibility. My failure in faith, my anxiety, my self-centeredness, my lack of joy become obstacles to the total outreach of the good news Christ came to share. Happily this is something the individual can do something about. Someone has said, "We kindle no fires from the burnt-out ashes of other mens' opinions." The kingdom of heaven is a pearl of great price (Matt. 13:46), and we must have the courage to make mature efforts if we are to expect mature results. The Christian who suffers from spiritual malnutrition can become more diligent in his communions and prayers; if loss of energy is the result of mental sloth, he can always give more time to self-discipline, study, and prayer. If unwillingness to forgive is at the heart of the problem, one only need remember how much forgiveness he himself needs. If the difficulty is a lack of confidence, preoccupation with things, or a secret sinful area of life, spiritual examination, perhaps with the assistance of a godly counselor, not only will clarify the nature of the problem but also suggest ways by which, with God's help, it may be resolved. This is where life is lived. Care must be taken to avoid rationalization, self-deception, and over-scrupulousness, and to resist the subtle demoniac suggestion that nothing matters in the long run. A good spiritual advisor, to paraphrase Gilbert and Sullivan, will let the solution fit the need. Additional humility is not needed by the man whose failure results from the lack of a proper self-esteem, and diligence is no remedy for the man already too busy to pray.

Doing the Work of an Evangelist

Carroll Simcox, editor of *The Living Church*, recently wrote, "If a church is not growing it is dying; growth is the result of faithfulness in mission and boldness in evangelism." God has a way in history of allowing things to go just so far and then he raises up new leadership, summons new laborers and pours out fresh power (Matt. 3:9). There are signs that God is beginning to effect such change in his church. The new ecumenical movement and the renewal of charismatic activity are signs of the times. There is increased awareness that evangelism is everybody's business and that the purpose of evangelism is not to make everybody a Baptist, an Episcopalian, a Roman Catholic, or a Pentecostal, but rather to share the Good News about Jesus Christ in such a way that those who hear will respond in thoughtful commitment, joyous prayer, loving relationships, and ongoing evangelism. The purpose of evangelism is not the creation of new power structures, the production of impressive statistics, or the adding of new burdens to already overburdened lives. The purpose of evangelism is the discovery, through Christ, of God as our true environment, the simplification of life (Matt. 6:22), and the restoring of broken relationships within a love-filled fellowship, the Christian church.

Here are some guidelines for those who are prepared to heed St. Paul's directive to "do the work of an evangelist" (2 Tim. 4:5):

1. be honest about your own commitment to Jesus Christ,
2. be loving,
3. be joyful,
4. pray much,
5. be open to the guidance and power of the Holy Spirit,
6. be informed,
7. avoid being defensive,

8. be patient, remembering your own intellectual and spiritual difficulties,
9. recognize that all truth belongs to God,
10. acknowledge that there are different ways in which God-loving persons interpret the Scriptures,
11. cultivate a variety of interests,
12. be prepared for misunderstanding but do not invite it,
13. do not make others uncomfortable,
14. be alert to unexpected opportunities,
15. be sure you remain related to the total church,
16. and for the ordained: be faithful to your ordination promises.

Those who write about evangelism sometimes make a distinction between "primary" and "secondary" evangelism. Primary evangelism is meant as personal, verbal witness to Jesus Christ in such a way as to call for response and commitment. Primary evangelism is not something which belongs exclusively to the clergy, who do have the additional advantage of their pulpits, but is an opportunity to witness belonging to all persons, all times, and all places. Secondary evangelism means witness by our love, the radiance of our joy, the courage with which we face difficulties, our obvious intellectual conviction, and a willingness to invite others to situations in which, always with their advance knowledge, they will be exposed to the verdict-demanding challenge of primary evangelism.

The distinction is valid because, while everybody can do evangelism, there are differences of gifts and different occasions. Those, therefore, who at a given time find that they can do only secondary evangelism need not have feelings of guilt, providing they are willing to do otherwise if God leads them in that direction; they should remember that when he wants them to do otherwise, he will give them ability equal to the task. Those who do primary evangelism ought always to remember that there is a sense in which their witness also is secondary. It is the Holy Spirit who is the ultimate witness to Christ!

Christ taught that at the Day of Judgment the final test will be the concern or lack of concern we had for others and the degree to which we manifested our caring in specific action (Matt. 25:31–36). Faith and action do not exist in tension, although there is evidence that such conflict was not unknown in biblical times (James 2).

Contemporary leadership, trapped in a crisis of faith, has found it easier to picket than to pray. When any denomination spends more of its national budget for a program designed to influence the internal affairs of industry than it spends on either education or evangelism, and when these latter programs are bankrupt, it is obvious that something has happened to its priorities. It has not been evil persons who were responsible for this, but good men and women, with prophetic concern, who unfortunately confused secular society with the kingdom of God (Matt. 11:11–15). Jesus taught that *being* is more fundamental than *doing* because it is from what we are that our good works proceed (Matt. 7:16 ff). Statistics tell the tragic consequences. Church membership has declined, and there has been a debilitating loss of financial support. What is worse, the laity, and not a few clergymen, have given up in despair; some have turned to non-christian religions for answers, to drugs for vision, and to sensuality for what is erroneously called discovery of self. This confusion about priorities on the part of leadership has left people not as much rebellious as bewildered, not as much indifferent as discouraged, not as much angry as confused. Some whose primary concern is evangelism have regarded social action as a spiritual "cop out" while the "activists" have dismissed evangelism as the "last gasp" of a remnant-minded orthodoxy. Both are wrong. Our Lord has given us the corrective principle, "These things ye ought to have done and not left the other undone" (Matt. 23:23). There can be no fulfillment of one without the other. Happily this old truth may be in the process of being rediscovered.

Education and Evangelism

There is confusion among Christians about the relationship of education and evangelism. They are neither substitutes one for the other or rival systems. Both are horizontal in action, but their goals are not the same. Evangelism seeks conscious, individual response at a particular time; education instructs as part of the converting process or after such response has been made, and there are those whose commitment is the result of an educational process and who probably are not aware of a specific time when conversion or a redirection of their loyalties occurred. The important thing is commitment to Jesus Christ. And Christians need to know that one has been made.

Failure to distinguish between evangelism, education, and social action can lead only to confusion and ineffectiveness. Put simply, education is instruction, social action a consequence of the fact that Christians care. Evangelism is always seeking a verdict. It asks, "What do you think about Jesus who is called *Christ?*" But the presentation is made in such a way as to invite the personal response, "He is the Christ, the son of the Living God!" (Matt. 16:16). The present church needs to remember that education and evangelism are not rivals; rather they complement one another. Most Christians owe their growth in Christ to many persons and processes. The members of the First Century Church in Corinth, which had more than its share of problems, had to be reminded that "Paul planted, Apollos watered, but God gave the increase" (1 Cor. 3:6).

While our present concern is primarily with evangelism, it may not be inappropriate to conclude this chapter with some observations about what commonly is called "Christian Education." The church has used many methods of instruction. It must be admitted that in spite of heroic efforts and the expenditure of vast sums of money its present programs are not very effective. A new approach is needed:

77

the purpose of Christian education is so to present the Christian faith as to strengthen those who are committed to Christ.

The purpose of Christian education is something more than the presentation of interesting but often unrelated Bible stories or the teaching of secular moral principles in the hope that little children will grow up and live good lives.

The concern of Christian education would seem to be the detailed presentation of the total Christian faith in such a way as to strengthen those who have made a commitment to Christ. The Lord Jesus promised that when the Holy Spirit came he would guide those who believed into all truth (John 16:13). He also promised that the Holy Spirit would come on one condition, obedience (John 14:16). Perhaps the time has come for a whole new curriculum based on "The Commandments of Christ," not as memory verses, a catechetical exercise, or a new legalism, but as the way a climate is created in which the Holy Spirit can work.

Christ gave some specific commandments:

1. follow me (Matt. 4:20, Mark 2:14 et. al.),
2. believe in me (John 14:1),
3. pray (Matt. 6:9),

4. do the Eucharist (1 Cor. 11:24–25),
5. love God (Mark 12:30),
6. love one another (John 13:35),
7. love your neighbor (Mark 12:31 et. al.),
8. forgive (Matt. 5:24, 6:14 et. al.),
9. relax (Matt. 6:25–34),
10. teach (Matt. 28:19),
11. baptize (Matt. 28:19 et. al.),
12. heal the sick (Matt. 10:8),
13. bear witness (Acts 1:8),
14. rejoice (John 16:33).

One does not become a doctor by studying hospital architecture, a baseball player by learning the color of major league uniforms, or a musician by reading the biographies of great composers. This, however, is the pedagogy upon which much religious instruction is based. The not-very-well-prepared Sunday school teacher begins by saying, "This morning, boys and girls, we shall learn the colors for the seasons of the Christian year, or we shall make a drawing which shows the parts of sanctuary or church, or we shall learn all about Jehu, a king of Israel whose claim to fame was that he drove furiously." What a waste of precious time! What an educational travesty!

It is in relevant instruction and faithful practice

that we are perfected. The study for Christians is how to respond effectively to the commandments of Christ. Otherwise the Holy Spirit cannot work in us, and we never shall truly know him whom we profess.

> *Send, we beseech thee, Almighty God, thy Holy Spirit into our hearts, that he may direct and rule us according to thy will, comfort us in all our afflictions, defend us from all error, and lead us into all truth; through Jesus Christ our Lord, who with thee and the same Holy Spirit liveth and reigneth, one God, world without end. Amen.*

—Book of Common Prayer

Prayer and the Personal God

Chapter Four

Prayer and the Personal God

Paradox and Perfection

The God of the Bible is personal; he is THE ONE WHO IS (Exod. 3:14). He has established an orderly universe which operates according to principles upon which we can depend and which sometimes we call "natural law." As part of this structure he has given man freedom of choice with the consequences such freedom entails, and prayer itself must be seen within the pattern of total creation—sharing both the potential and limitations such inclusion implies. All this is true, but it is also true that God is personal, and herein lies the paradox.

Sometimes two seemingly contradictory truths exist side by side and the conflict can be resolved only by a both/and approach rather than the more simplistic either/or. It is not a denial of what has been written earlier about the dynamics of prayer to suggest that caution must be exercised in any serious study of prayer lest it be reduced to a mechanistic and impersonal process, thus denying God that freedom of choice essential to personhood, a right we claim for ourselves and which he demonstrates in his dealings with men. In our thinking we must never exclude the possibility of personal and specific intervention above and beyond the normal patterns of prayer. Why, on occasion, God should so intervene is mystery. He is a God of compassion, but Christ's primary purpose was not the working of miracles; indeed, except when deeply moved, he seems to have avoided them (Mark 1:32–45 et. al.). On the other hand, he affirms his ability to respond. The case of the father whose son neither could hear nor speak is illustrative. "If thou canst," said the father, "Have compassion and help us," and Jesus replied, not without a suggestion of irritation, " 'If thou canst!' All things are possible to him that believes" (Mark 9:22–23).

Man's extremity is said to be God's opportunity.

There are times of darkness when all else proves inadequate, and we cry out with Job,

> I know that thou canst do all things;
> I have uttered that which I understand not,
> Things too wonderful for me,
> Wherefore I abhor myself
> And repent in dust and ashes (Job 42:1–6).

Many of the Psalms reflect the problem [22] with the general conclusion that, whatever the outcome, "It is good for me that I have been in trouble that I might learn thy statutes" (Ps. 119:71).

We have a great high priest who can respond in compassion because he has known our needs (Heb. 4:15, 7:25 et. al.). In the somewhat obscure and not altogether complimentary parable of a wronged widow and an indifferent magistrate (Luke 18:1–7), our Lord makes clear that, regardless of apparent results, we ought to continue to pray because in the long run God makes decisions for himself.

The paradox will not go away altogether. The extraordinary response remains extraordinary. Elijah was not sent to all the widows in Israel, but only to one in Zarephath, and Elisha did not heal all the lepers in the Middle East but only one, Naaman the Syrian (Luke 4:25–27). These are our Lord's own words. He himself did not heal all the infirm in Palestine. He continually emphasized that what is within is more important than any external circumstance (Matt. 10:28–31) and that God is one whom we can trust (Matt. 6:33, John 14:27 et. al.). Be persistent in prayer, "Leave all your anxiety with him; he careth for you" (1 Pet. 5:7).

The patient's condition was critical; the prognosis uncertain. His mood alternated between the kind of hope he had shared with others and the darkness of despair. It was a simple "get well" card as such cards go. It had cost a penny, perhaps; it had little artistry —two outstretched hands and a bit of Scripture which came as a message from heaven, "Underneath are the everlasting arms" (Deut. 33:27). In this life we never shall understand all the laws of the universe, including ourselves and how prayer operates, but God we can trust (Job 13:15).

> In heavenly love abiding,
> No change my heart shall fear,
> And safe is such confiding,

For nothing changes here.
The storm may roar without me,
My heart may low be laid;
But God is round about me,
And I am not afraid.[23]

Perfection or Integrity

THE ONE WHO IS and whom we trust is concerned
with a great deal more than what is technically called
"religion." He is the timeless Creator and tireless Sus-
tainer of a universe quite beyond our ability to comprehend and an ultimate perfection, in something
like but beyond a biological sense, for which all
things, including man, were made. He neither asks
nor expects the fawning adulation paganism gave its
deities (Ps. 50:9–14), but on the other hand, he in-
vites man to knowledge of and union with himself.
He is man's true environment, the One in whom we
live and have our being (Acts 17:28) and awareness
of whom is more than a new fad, the latest thing in
religious thought, or one more obligation to be met.
God alone is the perfect whole, the ultimate integrity
from which all meaning proceeds. The invitation is
to share in that totality of perfection which is derived
from him. Our Lord said, "This is eternal life that

they may know thee, the only true God, and Jesus Christ whom thou hast sent" (John 17:3); the New Testament thinks of "eternal life" not only as unending continuity but also perfection of content. This is the perfection, or integrity, to which we are called (John 17:21–23). This is our destiny.

That man is the climax of the creative process and of unique concern to God is what the biblical creation accounts are all about (Ps. 8:4–6). There is a great deal we do not know about the details of creation itself. The Hebrew word *soul* (Gen. 2:7) suggests something not unlike what in biology would be called a "mutation," a break with the past and a leap into the future, resulting in something so unique and different as to be in fact a new creature.

Most of man's problems are theological. This new creation failed to respond adequately to his total environment. To put it in secular language, his moral and spiritual capacity failed to keep step with his mental and physical development. As a result he lost (or failed to achieve) a necessary integrity. His wholeness was impaired which is what is meant by "the fall of man," and he became an alienated and lonely creature, fragmented within himself, rebellious, angry, destructive, having no identity with his fellow creatures or with the whole environment to which he belonged. Eventually God invaded history in the person of Christ to free man from the chain-reaction of evil resulting from this failure (John 8:32) and to restore the original integrity man had lost (John 10:10). The dictionary defines integrity (or perfection) as "the quality of being undivided, unimpaired, complete, or existing in a state comparable to an original condition." What could be more theological? What could be more biblical?

Man, thus restored, is enabled to go on toward a new wholeness or perfection. "Be ye therefore perfect as your Father in heaven is perfect" (Matt. 5:48). The perfection to which man is called is more than a code of conduct or an external legalism, and, while there are good reasons why man ought to worship, it is more than liturgical action. It has to do with man's very nature and, in a sense, is post-biological. St. Paul says much the same thing when he writes, "If any man put on Christ he is a new creation" (2 Cor. 5:17), and elaborates later to say, "There is a natural body and there is a spiritual body . . . but the glory of the terrestrial is one, and the glory of the celestial is another. . . . Howbeit that was not first which is spiritual but that which is natural, and afterward that which is spiritual" (1 Cor. 15).

St. Thomas Aquinas wrote that a perfect being is one who attains the end for which he (she) was created. Ultimate perfection, or integrity, exists only in God himself. Man was created to be "friends with God" [24] and therefore we realize our ultimate wholeness or integrity only as we are one with him. The purpose of atone-ment is at-onement, that he may live in us and we in him (John 14:20).

The life of perfection, the life of integrity, also sometimes called in theology "the unitive way" [25] is both a foretaste of future glory we shall know in heaven and also an actualization of the freedom and fulfillment God intends those who love him to have in this world.

The kingdom of God is not limited to the religious professionals. There was profound truth in Jenny Lind's statement, "I sing unto God." [26] St. Paul makes the same point when he says, "Whatsoever you do, whether in word or deed, do all in the name of the Lord Jesus" (Col. 3:17). Those who are beginning to live the unitive way do different things, have different backgrounds and are of different ages and sexes, some come with great promise and others with limited gifts. God accepts them all. There are no barriers to holiness except those within the human will and heart. To suggest that the so-called secular vocations involve a kind of second class relationship to God is blasphemous, as saints in every generation remind us.

The integrated life continues to be involved in the business of everyday living, but as we grow in aware-ness, we discover gifts and grace we would not have otherwise—freedom from fear, guilt, anxiety and self-centeredness; freedom to be one's self, which means to act rather than merely react, to think, to love, to laugh, to dream, to work, to play; freedom to be open and patient in our relationships because we no longer are "threatened," and a new capacity to rise above frustration, danger, anxiety, and even death. We have learned at the deepest levels of our consciousness that "If the son shall make us free we are free indeed!" (John 8:38).

A legitimate response to so great a promise is to say, "All this is fine; now tell us how it is achieved." It is not achieved but given; we need only meet the conditions of obedience, prayer, and simple trust. God will do the rest.

Jesus said, "If you love me keep my commandments." [27] He promised life through the work of the Holy Spirit—the kind of integrated, total life with which we are concerned. This life, however, is not our reward for obedience or something we can earn. To obey is to meet the conditions necessary to make us receptive, to create a climate within which he can work. The Christmas hymn is correct, "Where meek souls will receive him still, the Christ child enters in." [28]

We must pray. It is prayer which leads us to an effective awareness of the "breadth and length and depth and heighth of love as revealed in Christ" (Eph. 3:18); no one story universe this! It is in prayer and especially in the prayer of silence that God speaks to us and that a true awareness of his presence is achieved. He who learns to practice the prayer of silence will discover to his surprise the joyous certainty of the presence of God. He will *know for himself* the One in whom he has believed (2 Tim. 1:12).

Finally there is the matter of trust. The Book of Job and the Epistle to the Hebrews particularly remind us that God sometimes uses our disappointments and sufferings as schoolmasters to teach us compassion, patience, and trust. [29] This is not to say that God sends trouble (James 1:13) but that it is possible to bring good out of evil and that misfortune can be a doorway to growth. Sometimes in darker moments we cry, "Why did this happen to me?," but morning comes and we learn with St. Paul that "God will not let us be tempted beyond that which we are able to endure" (1 Cor. 10:13) and that we have grown as a result of our grief. It is in life's contrasts that we find the wonder of wholeness and the meaning of praise. To hear him say, "I am your Savior, trust me" and to respond in hope is to be united with him who said, "Cheer up! I have overcome the world!" (John 16:33).

All this makes sense only as we believe in Christ in the traditional sense, and as we are willing that the Holy Spirit should work in us. It is quite incomprehensible otherwise (John 14:17). It is only as we adapt to our larger environment that we recover the integrity which has been lost. The history of life on this planet teaches us that the future belongs only to those who are capable of such response.

Prayer is essential to the total process. It unites the self with God, unifies the one who prays within himself, and relates persons to one another in ways which are loving and creative. Prayer is the climate in which we relate to God, who is our true environment, and thus find the freedom and fullness of personhood he intends us to have.

The person who has discovered the consequences of prayer for himself will want to pray; he will also want to share his discovery with others, which is what is meant by evangelism.

Come down, O Love divine,
Seek thou this soul of mine,
And visit it with thine own ardor glowing;
O Comforter, draw near,
Within my heart appear,
And kindle it, thy holy flame bestowing.

O let it freely burn,
Till earthly passions turn
To dust and ashes in its heat consuming;
And let the glorious light
Shine ever on my sight,
And clothe me round, the while my path illuming.

And so the yearning strong,
With which the soul will long
Shall far out pass the power of human telling;
For none can guess its grace,
Till he become the place
Wherein the Holy Spirit makes his dwelling.[30]

Notes

Notes

1. The "Jesus Prayer," a favorite devotion in the Eastern Church: "Lord Jesus Christ, Son of God, have mercy on me, a sinner."
2. The traditional four steps in meditation also are described as: "Jesus in the eyes, Jesus in the head, Jesus in the heart, Jesus in the hands" or, less specifically Christian as: "The subject, considerations, affections, resolutions."
3. Alexis Carrell, frequently-quoted late Fellow of the American College of Surgeons; born 1873; recipient Norduff-Jung Medal for Cancer Research and Nobel prize winner for the development of a technique for suturing blood vessels.
4. Adapted from Montgomery's nineteenth century hymn, composed in response to Edward Bickersteth's *Treatise on Prayer*, 1818.
5. The General Electric Company, Schenectady, N.Y., about 1936. For a recent and sophisticated article on the principle see: McElheney, *New York Times*, Oct. 10, 1975.
6. See *Oxford Dictionary of the Christian Church*, second edition, page 80.

7. Mark 14:36, Romans 8:15, Galatians 4:6 where, interestingly, it always is translated for the benefit of readers who might not have understood Aramaic. Also see Westminister, *Dictionary of the Bible*, page 2.

8. Contemporary scholarship generally agrees that a number of older documents were incorporated into the Penteteuch, i.e., the first five books of the Old Testament, also known as The Law or Torah. One of the earliest of these literary strands is the so-called "J Document," thus named because it uses the Hebrew word JHVH or "Jahveh" for the name of God. The J Document took its final form before the eighth century B.C. The more modern name for God, "Jehovah" results from a combination of the consonants of the sacred name, which out of reverence Judaism does not like to pronounce, with the vowels of the more familiar word, ADONAI or "Lord" thus providing a substitute word.

9. Concern for the poor is a basic tenet of both the Old and the New Testaments: Psalms 34; 41; Job 34:18; Luke 1:46, et. al.

10. Laing, *The Politics of Experience*. Middlesex, England: Penguin Books, Ltd, 1967.

11. 2 Corinthians 5:17. *The Living Bible* rendition is especially appropriate.

12. The familiar hymn written by William How in 1867 probably was inspired by the exhibition of Holman Hunt's popular painting, first exhibited in 1867.

13. The word "grace" (Greek, *Xaris*) means something freely given, an overplus, as it were, without which a desired objective could not be achieved.

14. See Luke 9:24. The Greek word is *"psyche."*

15. *The Dynamics of Human Adjustment*, Appleton-Century, 1946.

16. Maurice Strong, Canadian businessman and Executive Director U.N. Environmental Program.

17. Teilhard de Chardin, *The Phenomonon of Man*, New York: Harper & Row, 1959, p. 246.

18. ——— *The Phenomenon of Man*, p. 248. Others refer to this as a "Psychozoic Age."

19. A Russian Orthodox priest of the nineteenth century.

20. See also Romans 5:10; the Greek word is *Katallasso*, hence "Catalyst."

21. Taylor, *Perspective in Education, Religion and the Arts*, Brockport, N.Y.: State University of

New York, 1969, Vol. 3, page 6. "I recommend as an invitation to intellectual disaster a visit to the meetings of the American Philosophical Association in session. There the intellect does not survive for the bureaucracy. The papers are, as I have already suggested, written for other philosophers. . . ." Dr. Taylor would have a similar reaction if he were to visit the average church synod, conference or convention.

22. Among the Psalms particularly illustrating this conclusion are: 6, 13, 18, 22, 23, 30, 31, 38, 42, 61, 63, 71, 86, 91, 103, 116, 130.

23. A. L. Waring, 1850.

24. The Rev. Roland F. Palmer, S.S.J.E., a well-known Anglican mission preacher, describes religion as "being friends with God."

25. Ascetic theology notes three levels in the spiritual life: the Purgative Way, the Illuminative Way, and the Unitive Way; the meanings are obvious.

26. A popular singer brought to the United States by P. T. Barnham and known as "The Swedish Nightingale." She died in 1887.

27. See Chapter 3.

28. Verse 3, Phillips Brooks' popular Christmas Hymn, "O Little Town of Bethlehem." Inci-

dentally the Hebrew word, *Bethlehem* means "House of Bread"; cf. John 6:48–51, 1 Corinthians 11:23–24; "Remembrance" in its common usage is a not altogether adequate translation.

29. See Heb. 12:1–6.
30. Bianco da Siena, fifteenth century church hymnal translation.

model's auto Repair

05/
led